AF449458

The
ROCK-CUT
TEMPLES OF INDIA

MAVEN BOOKS

The
ROCK-CUT
TEMPLES OF INDIA

James Fergusson

MAVEN BOOKS

Chennai   New Delhi

This edition has been published in india by arrangement with Carson Books, UK

ISBN 9789355275721   Maven Books

All rights reserved   No. 44, Nallathambi Street,
Printed and bound in India   Triplicane, Chennai 600 005

MJP 1575   © Publishers, 2023

Publisher :   C. Janarthanan

Publisher's Note

The legacy of a country is in its varied cultural heritage, historical literature, developments in the field of economy and science. The top nations in the world are competing in the field of science, economy and literature. This vast legacy has to be conserved and documented so that it can be bestowed to the future generation. The knowledge of this legacy is slowly getting perished in the present generation due to lack of documentation.

Keeping this in mind, the concern with retrospective acquiring of rare books has been accented recently by the burgeoning reprint industry. Maven Books is gratified to retrieve the rare collections with a view to bring back those books that were landmarks in their time.

In this effort, a series of rare books would be republished under the banner, "Maven Books". The books in the reprint series have been carefully selected for their contemporary usefulness as well as their historical importance within the intellectual. We reconstruct the book with slight enhancements made for better presentation, without affecting the contents of the original edition.

Most of the works selected for republishing covers a huge range of subjects, from history to anthropology. We believe this reprint edition will be a service to the numerous researchers and practitioners active in this fascinating field. We allow readers to experience the wonder of peering into a scholarly work of the highest order and seminal significance.

MAVEN BOOKS

PREFACE.

DURING a lengthened residence in India it was my good fortune to be able to visit in succession all the principal groups of Rock-cut Temples which were then known to exist in that country.

In 1836 those of Cuttack were first examined. In 1838 an extended tour was made for the purpose of exploring those of Western India, and in 1841 the investigation was completed by a visit to those of Mahavellipore, in the Madras Presidency The intervals that elapsed between these several dates were useful for correcting the vagueness of first impressions, and in enabling me to fill up the gaps in my knowledge of Indian architecture, by examining cotemporary structural buildings, and studying other cognate sources of information.

The results of these investigations were embodied in a paper which was read to the Royal Asiatic Society in 1843, and published in the Eighth Volume of its Journal.

This paper was afterwards republished in 1845, accompanied by nineteen lithographic plates, in folio, illustrating the principal types of Rock-cut Architecture in India.

In consequence of the interest which these publications excited among those interested in the study of Indian Antiquities, a memorial was addressed to the Court of Directors of the East India Company, praying them to take steps to prevent further desecration and destruction of these venerable monuments of the past, and above all to appoint some one to make drawings of the fast perishing Frescoes of Ajunta, before decay and the recklessness of Tourists had entirely obliterated them.

One result of these representations was, that Captain,—now Major Gill, was appointed to copy the paintings in Ajunta; a task for which he proved himself thoroughly competent, by the artistic skill displayed in the copies of these paintings which he has sent home, as well as by the truthfulness and fidelity which pervade all he has done.

The pictures sent home by Major Gill during the first few years of his residence at Ajunta are now exhibited in the Indian Court of the Crystal Palace at Sydenham, and convey a perfect idea of the style of the paintings at Ajunta; but unfortunately they have not been accompanied by any explanation, or any indication of the localities in which they are found. The only attempt to elucidate their history, which has yet been published, will be found in Mrs. Spier's " Life in Ancient India," published in 1856.

For many years past no further drawings have reached this country, but instead, Major Gill sent home in the spring of this year to Mr. Layard nearly two hundred stereoscopic views of Indian subjects.

Preface.

About one-half these were scenes of the chase, of Indian
life, and illustrations of the Mahometan buildings and of the
scenery in the neighbourhood of Ajunta. Of the remaining
half, many were duplicates, but those forming the illustrations
of the present volume, have been selected as being all those in
the collection which could fairly be considered as representing
Rock-cut Architecture.

The text which accompanies them is not intended to be a
complete and scientific elucidation of the subject. Those who
desire fuller information are referred to the works mentioned
above : but it is hoped that it is sufficient to render the subject
of each Photograph intelligible. This seems to be all that is
necessary, for the Photographs tell their own story far more
clearly than any form of words that could be devised, and even
without the text they form by far the most perfect and satis-
factory illustration of the ancient architecture of India which
has yet been presented to the Public.

JAMES FERGUSSON.

20, LANGHAM PLACE,
   October, 1863.

CONTENTS.

CAVES OF AJUNTA.

Contents.

Contents.

CAVES OF ELLORA.

<h1 style="text-align:center">INTRODUCTION.</h1>

THERE are few among the monuments of antiquity regarding whose history or uses so much uncertainty prevailed, till a very recent period, as those known as the rock-cut temples of India. When Europeans first became acquainted with them, they were so struck by their monolithic grandeur, and the apparent eternity of duration that resulted from it, that they jumped at once to the conclusion that they must be among the most ancient monuments of the world, rivalling in this respect, as was then supposed, even those of Egypt. There was also a mystery hanging over their deserted condition, added to the fact that almost all of them were situated in remote and lonely valleys, or cut into the bare mountain-side; which, with other circumstances, conspired to render them the most attractive, as they certainly were the grandest, relics of the arts of the ancient Hindoo races.

In consequence of all this, the wildest theories were adopted with regard to their antiquity and the purposes for which they were originally intended. These might have continued in vogue till the present day had not James Prinsep, between the years 1830 and 1840, opened a new era in our knowledge of Indian antiquities, and introduced new modes of investigation, which soon led to most important results.

Among the first fruits of his labours was the decipherment of the Great Buddhist inscriptions, which exist all over Northern India, from beyond the Indus at Kapur di Giri to the shores of the Bay of Bengal at Cuttack.

This discovery led to a thorough investigation of the Buddhist literature of Ceylon by the Hon. Mr. Turnour, and the consequent fixation of the date of the birth of Sakya Muni, the founder of that faith, in or about the year 623 B.C., and of his death eighty years later, in 543. It was also then ascertained that Buddhism did not become a prevalent, still less a state religion, till 300 years afterwards, in the reign of Asoka. As all the earlier excavations belong to this faith, an initial date was thus obtained, beyond which it was impossible to carry back the antiquity of any of the rock-cut temples then known or since brought to light. Subsequent researches have more and more confirmed the conclusions then arrived at ; and there seems no reason for doubting but that the whole series of Indian Rock-cut Temples were excavated in the fourteen centuries which elapsed between the time when Dasaratha, the grandson of Asoka, excavated the " Milkmaid's Cave " in Behar, about 200 years B.C., and the completion of the Indra Subha by Indradyumna at Ellora, in the twelfth century after our era.

As might naturally be expected from their locality, the oldest group of these caves is that at Raja Griha in Behar, being close to the original seat of Buddhism, and where it first rose into importance. They extend from 200 B.C. to the destruction of the Andhra dynasty in the fifth century of our era.

Next to these is the Cuttack series, beginning about the same time, but ending earlier in so far as Buddhism is concerned, but continued through a Jaina series of much more modern date. These are the only two groups known to exist in Bengal.

On the western side of India, the Cave at Karli is apparently not only the oldest, but the finest known to exist. It is situated on what is now, and probably was then, the great highroad between the plains of the Deccan and the Harbour of Bombay, which we know to have been an important Buddhist locality, from the number of caves that still exist around it. But the most complete and interesting series known is that of Ajunta, which are fully illustrated in this volume. They extend from the first century B.C. to the tenth or eleventh A.D. and present every variety of style of Buddhist art prevalent in India during that important period.

Next in importance to these is the well-known group at Ellora, consisting of three series :—First, a Buddhist group, which may probably be as old as the seventh, but more probably belongs to the eighth or ninth, century. After these comes a Hindoo series, lasting through the next two or three centuries, and closing with a Jaina group of the eleventh or twelfth. They form thus a singular contrast with those at Ajunta, where all belong to one religion ; though it may be a question whether the variety of the one series is not as interesting as the uniformity of the other.

Besides this, there is a very important and interesting series of caves at Kennari in the island of Salsette, in Bombay Harbour— wholly Buddhist, and of various ages—and the well-known Hindoo cave of Elephanta, of the eighth or ninth century.

In the Ghâts above Bombay there is another important series, at Juneer ; a Buddhist group at Baug, in Malwa ; and one partly Buddhist and partly Brahmanical at Dhumnar, and several others less known, and which yet remain to be examined and described.

Only one important group is known to exist in the Madras Presidency, that at Mahavellipore, on the coast, south of Madras. They are comparatively modern, and may be as late as the thirteenth century of our era. They present a curious mixture of Brahmanical and Buddhist forms of architecture, but cannot bear comparison either in extent or interest with those existing in the Bengal or Bombay Presidencies.

Altogether, it has been calculated there may be in India 1,000 excavations of this class—nine-tenths of which are Buddhist, and the remaining 100 divided between the Brahmanical and Jaina religions. They thus form not only the most numerous, but the most interesting series of architectural remains existing in India before the Mahomedan Conquest. In fact, they are the only ones that serve to illustrate the Arts or History of the period to which they belong. The structural monuments erected during the early centuries of our era are scarce and widely scattered over the whole area of the country, and few even of these are in the state in which they were originally erected ; whereas one of the great merits of cave architecture is that it remains unchanged and unchangeable during the whole period of its existence.

In order to understand what has just been said and a great deal of what is to follow, it is necessary to bear in mind that three great phases of religious faith have succeeded one another in India in historical times. The first was that of the immigrating Aryans—an elemental fire-worship, as far removed from superstition or idolatry as any human faith well can be. We know it only from the Vedas, and from its analogy with the fire-worship of the ancient Persians; for no stranger visited India during its prevalence who has left us an account of what he saw, and no monument or material records remain by which it could be judged. We have every reason, however, to suppose that it continued pure and undefiled till the period when it was superseded by Buddhism, some three centuries before our era.

We have only slight means of guessing what the religion of the aboriginal Indians may have been in early times, but it seems clear that Buddhism was little else than a raising up of the aboriginal casteless Hindoos to a temporary supremacy over the aristocratic Aryans. When Buddhism broke down in India, of which we have symptoms as early as the sixth century A. D., it was succeeded in some parts of Western India by the religion of Jaina; a form of faith that may have existed in obscurity contemporaneously with the other, but only came to light on its extinction.

What really replaced it, however, was the modern Brahmanical worship of Siva and Vishnu. This was apparently the religion of some of the original inhabitants of the country with whom the effete remnant of the old Brahmanical Aryans allied themselves, in order to overthrow the Buddhists. In this they succeeded; but this most unholy alliance has given birth to one of the most monstrous superstitions the world now knows, but which generally prevails at the present day over the whole peninsula of India.

So far as we know, the Aryans built no permanent buildings in India. Their pure religion required no stately ceremonies, and consequently no temples. The climate is so temperate, that palatial structures were only necessary for the display of passing pageantry; and it also happens that where races of men are not in the habit of building temples or tombs, their residences are more remarkable for temporary convenience than they are for permanent magnificence.

Architectural magnificence was, on the contrary, a necessity with the Turanian natives ; and one of the most interesting points brought out by the study of the caves is the fact, that the earliest are mere petrifactions of wooden buildings. The mortices, the tenons, and every form of wooden construction, is repeated in the rock in the earliest caves ; and frequently even the woodwork still remains as if placed there to support the mountain, instead of being merely intended to recall the structure of the metal covered or boarded roof from which it was copied.

The same thing occurred in Lycia, where all the earliest tombs are in like manner repetitions in stone of wooden structures, and in both instances it appears that it was the Greeks who taught the natives how to use the more permanent materials. At all events, the earliest monuments we know in India, the lâts of Asoka, are adorned with Greek ornaments, evidently borrowed from the Bactrian Greeks of Central Asia, and in the earlier caves there $_{is}$ not one single form that suggests lithic architecture ; every form is essentially wooden, and frequently interchanging with wood itself.

All the Buddhist caves we know of belong to one of two classes. They are either Viharas or Monasteries, or they are Chaitya caves or churches,—the former being, as might be expected, by far the most numerous. The oldest Viharas consist of one cell only ; little hermitages, in fact, for the residence of a

Fig. 1

PLAN OF VIHARA AT UDYAGIRI. SCALE 25 FEET TO 1 INCH.

single ascetic. In the next class they were extended to a long verandah, with one long cell behind it, as in the example, Fig. 1. As these had, however, several doors opening outwards, they probably were divided by partitions into cells internally.

In the third, and by far the most numerous class, Fig. 2, the cell expands into a hall, generally with pillars in the centre ; and around this the cells of the monks are arranged, the abbot or prior generally occupying cells at either end of the verandah.

Fig. 2.

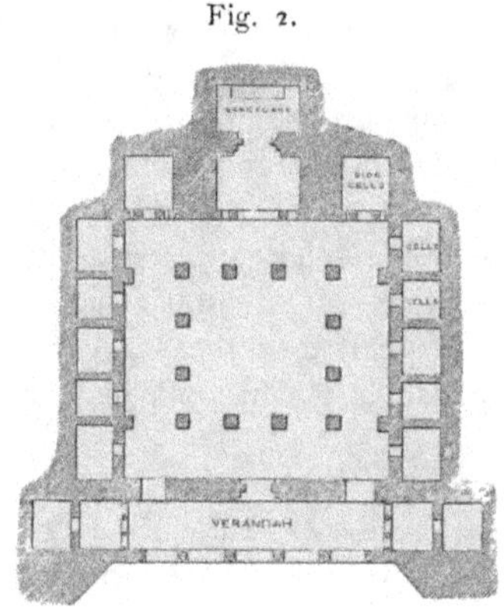

PLAN OF VIHARA NO. 2. AT AJUNTA.   SCALE 50 FEET TO 1 INCH

In ancient times, no sculpture or images were introduced into the Viharas ; but as early, certainly, as the first or second century of our era we find a chapel always facing the principal entrance, and in it an image of Buddha : afterwards side chapels were added, with images of saints ; and in those groups of caves which had no Chaitya cave attached to them we find a dagopa, or stone altar, occupying the chapel in the centre.

Chaitya caves, on the contrary, are always exclusively devoted to ceremonial worship, and in every feature correspond with the choir of a Romanesque or Basilican church, the climate apparently enabling them to dispense with the nave, or place of assembly for the laity.   As mentioned above, the typical example of this class is the great cave of Karli, of which is represented in plan on woodcut Fig. 3.

Externally there was always a porch or music gallery, more or less developed ; within this, a feature corresponding with our rood-screen.   This is always covered with sculpture, and access was obtained to the choir through one or three doors with which it was pierced. Internally, over the entrance, is the part corresponding with the rood-loft, and over this is the great window or chancel arch, through which light is admitted to the building.

Fig. 3.

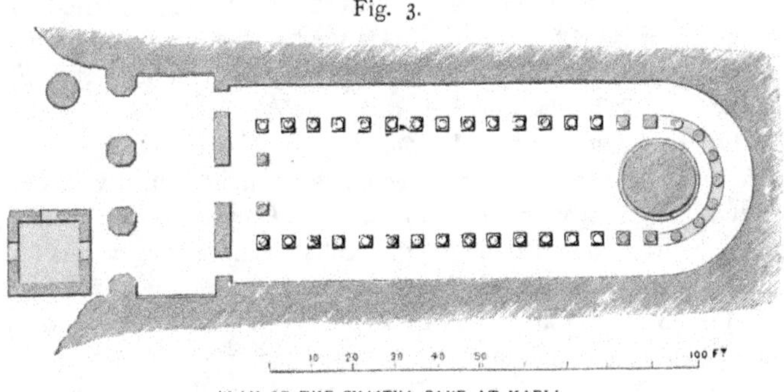

PLAN OF THE CHAITYA CAVE AT KARLI.

The end, opposite the entrance, always terminates in an apse, the centre of which is occupied by the dagopa, or stone altar, a simulated tomb, containing, or supposed to contain, a relic of Buddha, or of some of his saints.

Fig. 4

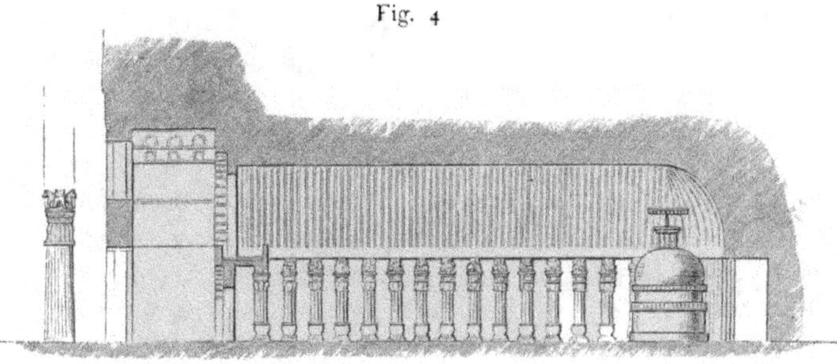

SECTION OF THE CHAITYA CAVE AT KARLI.

The whole is always surrounded by an aisle or procession path, separated from the choir by a range of pillars; over that is generally a triforium belt, not pierced, but ornamented either by painting or sculpture. From this belt springs the semicircular roof. In the oldest Chaityas, this was always ornamented with wooden ribs attached to the rock, and at Karli, woodcut Fig. 4, these still remain. At Kennari, the wooden tenons still stick in the rock ; but in most cases they are replaced by stone ribs cut out of the rock.

As the Brahmans excavated caves only in order to signalize their triumph over their enemies the Buddhists, and had no real purpose to guide them, their excavations are more varied in character, and not so easily classified. Generally speaking, however, they too may be divided into two classes—Pseudo Viharas and Temples.

The first of these resemble true monasteries at first sight, being caves with flat roofs supported by pillars, sometimes nearly similar to Buddhist excavations in arrangement. They are distinguished, however, from these, by having no cells or any arrangements for residence, the wall spaces between the pillars being invariably occupied by sculpture or niches for its reception ; and instead of the chapel, or dagopa, there is generally either a small temple or a figure of Siva or Vishnu. Even without sculpture, however, there are peculiarities of plan in Brahmanical excavations which at once betray their origin to any one familiar with the archi-tectural arrangement of Buddhist Viharas.

The Brahmanical temples are still more unlike the Buddhist examples, as these are invariably exteriors, and have consequently no meaning when cut in the rock.   In almost every case they have also the disadvantage of standing in a pit, the rock being dug out all round, leaving them in the midst of the excavation. The one exception to this rule is the example of the Raths at Mahavellipore. There the Brahmans found a group of granite boulders lying on the seashore, and have carved them into the form of temples, having all the appearance of structural edifices with the advantage of monolithic durability; but the parts being all copied from edifices constructed with small stones, no apparent grandeur of effect results from this cause. The Kylas at Ellora and the temple at Dhumnar are, on the contrary, hid from view externally, and when looked at from above lose half the effect due to their dimensions. When standing in the pit, however, and looking up at them, there is something in the seclusion, and an effect of eternity in the simple wall of rock enclosing the richly-carved temple, which goes far to redeem these faults, and renders them, on the whole, much more impressive than structural temples of even greatly increased dimensions.

The Jaina temples are so few as hardly to require classification, and have no architectural peculiarities by which they can be distinguished. Their arrangements partake principally of that of the Brahmanical caves; indeed, it is only by their sculpture that they can be distinguished from them. They are interesting, however, from the circumstance of their belonging to the most florid period of Hindoo art; and they were also fortunate in being excavated at a time when even the Brahmans had become so familiar with monolithic architecture as to have abandoned most of the faults inherent in direct imitation of structural edifices.

It is in vain now to speculate on what may first have induced the inhabitants of Behar to excavate temples in the hard granite rocks of their country, or those of Cuttack in the coarse sand-stone of Khandagiri. It may have been a familiarity with those of Egypt, as we know from his inscriptions, that Asoka had formed alliances with Ptolemy of Egypt, and Megas, probably of Cyrene; and to a people wholly without permanent monuments as the Hindoos then were, the temptation to imitate the rock-cut monuments of these countries was great. What, however, really led to their ultimate extension was the singularly favourable nature of the rocks in Western India for the purpose.

From the valley of the Nerbudda to that of the Kistnah, the whole country consists of horizontally stratified trap rocks perfectly homogeneous in character. Occasionally, however, strata intervene of harder texture than the rest, giving that curious steplike character which distinguishes the hill forts of India. Whether harder or softer, it is free from faults and cracks, and so uniform in character, that the architect feels the most perfect confidence in finding a suitable material, however deeply he may penetrate.

The Tapty is one of the few streams which have cut through the upper crust of this formation, and opened for itself a deep and wide valley through it, pursuing a western course. On either side of this great valley numerous ravines or cracks extend for some miles into the plateau.

Introduction.

It is in one of these ravines, on the southern side of the valley of the Tapty, about three miles from the outer edge or ghât, that the Caves of Ajunta are situated.

In order to render the following description of these caves intelligible, it is necessary, before proceeding further, to explain how the numbers by which they are known came to be attached to them. When I visited the caves in 1839, some of them had names, but such as neither indicated their age nor the purposes for which they were excavated, and these were applied so loosely that the guides frequently gave the same name first to one cave and then to another. To avoid all difficulty, I numbered them like houses in a street, beginning with the most northern, or the cave furthest down the stream, and proceeded to No. 27, the last accessible cave at the southern end.

According to this arrangement, the oldest group consists of the 9th, 10th, 11th, and 12th, and the series becomes more and more modern very nearly in the exact ratio on which it diverges on either hand from this central group. Thus the group from No. 13 to No. 19 comes next in age, and beyond these the northern Caves, Nos. 1 to 7; and the southern, Nos. 20 to 27, are probably cotemporary or nearly so. The earliest Viharas, Nos. 11 and 12, were probably excavated in the century which preceded the Christian era—they may be older; while the excavation of No. 1 and No. 26 probably did not long precede the first Mahomedan Conquest.

It may also be remarked, that Nos. 9, 10, 19, and 26 are Chaitya, or Church caves; the remaining twenty-three are Viharas. There are no Brahmanical caves at Ajunta, but some sculpture that approaches very nearly to that religion in character, and may have been excavated either after the caves were abandoned by their original occupants, or during some period of temporary supremacy.

CAVES OF AJUNTA.

BRIDGE AND TOWN OF AJUNTA.

A T the head of the ravine in which the Caves are situated stands Ajunta, a picturesque but thinly inhabited town, at one time well known in our annals in consequence of its being situated near the field of battle of Assaye. The Bara Durree or Palace was then used as a field hospital, and the graves of the officers who fell are still to be seen on the plateau opposite it, on the right of the picture.

At this point the stream is crossed by a bridge of ten arches, which serves also to dam back the waters of the river so as to form a reservoir above the bridge. A little farther down a second obstruction forms an artificial lake in front of the Bara Durree, as shown in the photograph, and adds at the same time to the height of the first of a series of falls, by which the river descends to that part of the ravine where the Caves are situated.

HEAD OF RAVINE.—AJUNTA.

THE town of Ajunta is situated on the level of the plains of the Deccan, on the top of the Ghat. The Caves are situated about 200 feet lower down, at the bottom of a second stratum of the trap rocks. Half way between them a platform of harder rock divides the height into two nearly equal strata of 100 feet each.

After leaping over the two artificial obstructions shewn in the last view, the river descends by numerous small falls through the first stratum in a course of about two miles long. It then reaches the edge of the lower platform, over which it falls by seven short leaps, in a narrow space just to the right of the rocks shown in the view, which close the upper end of the lower ravine.

GENERAL VIEW OF CAVES.—AJUNTA.

IMMEDIATELY below the rocks shown on the last photograph, the river makes a sudden bend to the left, on the outer sweep of which the Caves are situated.

This view is interesting as showing the two great platforms of trap-rock of which this country is composed. The upper, perfectly flat, forms the plain of the Deccan. The lower, equally horizontal, is the one in which the caves are situated. The river Tapty flows over a third, which it also cuts through lower down. And above all these three is an upper stratum, but only existing in detached horizontal fragments, which give so peculiar a form to the celebrated hill forts of this part of India.

CAVES No. 1 TO No. 14.—AJUNTA.

THIS view represents the principal and oldest group of the Ajunta Caves. The two Chaitya Caves, with their great semicircular windows, seen in the centre of the view, are Nos. 9 and 10. The two oldest Viharas, Nos. 11 and 12, are those on the left of these two, and the view extends on the right nearly to No. 1, which terminates the series in this direction.

The demarcation of the two strata of trap is very clearly shown in this view, as also the nature of the scrub jungle, which covers the hills in every direction in this country, forming an immense forest, but without a single tree of anything like magnificent dimensions.

THE FIRST SEVEN CAVES AT AJUNTA

———

THE lower or northern group of Caves, extending from the two older Chaitya caves seen in the last view to the commencement of the series. The first Cave on the left of the picture is that known as No. 7.   Next to it is the two-storied cave numbered as 6.   No. 4 is seen on the same level as its lower storey, and on the level of its upper storey are seen the three magnificent Viharas known as Nos. 1, 2, and 3.

SOUTHERN END OF THE SERIES OF CAVES.—AJUNTA.

THIS view is taken from the verandah of Cave No. 16, looking south-ward, and represents the opposite end of the series from that of the last illustration. The Chaitya Cave seen in the extreme left is No. 26. Those next it on its right are the unfinished Viharas Nos. 23 and 24 ; and in the centre of the view is that known as No. 21.

As will be observed, the Caves here are very much higher above the bottom of the ravine than those towards the other end, especially those in the centre. This arose apparently from their architects following the vein of rock, the texture of which seemed most suitable for their purpose.

THE OLDEST GROUP OF CAVES.—AJUNTA.

A LARGER view of the oldest or central group, comprising the two Chaitya Caves, Nos. 9 and 10, and interesting as explaining why this spot was chosen for the earliest excavation. As is seen from the picture, the rock here is smoother and more perpendicular than anywhere else, and carries its smoothness down almost to the bottom of the ravine. To the right and left the platform of rock rises considerably, and the Caves are situated on a ledge, which was probably broader in former times, but is now hardly passable in places. It is only by getting on the terrace at this point that the outer excavations are reached. Apparently, there never was any other ascent to any of the Caves but at this spot.

THE OLDEST CHAITYA CAVE AT AJUNTA.

THE façade of (No. 9), the smaller of the two old Chaitya Caves, shows tolerably clearly the imitation of wooden forms in this style of archi-tecture, as it came into use before the Christian Era.

Within the great arch, on either side, are two upright posts, on which the two principal rafters rest. The broken end of one of these is seen on the right. Below, five smaller are placed horizontally, and between the two prin-cipals, seven are arranged perpendicularly.

The great flat ogee was probably originally painted, and represents a sort of barge board terminating the gable. It probably assumed this form because it was necessary to have a ridge to the roof to throw off the rain.

On the face of the rib lining the interior of the arch may be seen the incised footings into which a wooden framework was inserted, partially closing the great arch. Its form may be seen copied in the niches below.

To the left is some sculpture of much more modern date, but from the head of the principal figure having been destroyed, it is difficult to make out whom it represents. The dimensions of this Cave internally are 45 ft. by 23 ft.

CHAITYA CAVE No. 10.—AJUNTA.

INTERIOR view of the Chaitya Cave No. 10, rather more than twice the dimensions of the last, being 94 ft. 6 in. in depth, by 41 ft. 3 in. in width. There are twenty-nine pillars surrounding the nave, all plain octagons without bases or capitals, but covered with chunam and painted. Above these is the triforium belt, which was also painted, but very few traces of this remain. On the roof is still seen the markings of the timber framing that once adorned it. Being actually of wood they have perished, but having been copied in stone in the side aisles, they still remain there. The dagopa also shows marks of the wooden and plaster decorations that once ornamented it. The tee, or square relic casket, on its summit, being cut in the rock, still retains its original form, but the umbrella which once crowned it, being of wood, has perished, and nothing remains to tell of its existence here but the mortice into which it was originally stepped.

THE OLDEST VIHARA.—AJUNTA.

THIS and the following view, represent the interior of No. 12, the oldest Vihara or Monastery at Ajunta, and from the analogy with other similar excavations bearing inscriptions, was excavated almost certainly anterior to the Christian Era, though how long before it cannot now be determined.

It consists of a square hall, 36 ft. 7 in. each way without any pillars or internal supports. It has three cells on the right-hand side as you enter, and four cells on each of the other two faces. Towards the face of the rock it has one doorway, with a window on each side.

It is peculiar at Ajunta, from having no central cell opposite the entrance, and no image or object of worship of any sort. In this respect it resembles the old Cuttack and Behar Caves, none of which have any images in their interiors, though the practice was apparently universal in the West soon after the age at which these earliest caves were excavated.

T^HE OLDEST VIHARA.—AJUNTA.

T^HE only ornaments in this Cave are seven horse-shoe arches on the left-hand side and front, four over the doorways of the cells, and three over false doorways or niches between. On the right-hand side, however, where the residence of the abbot seems to have been, there are only three cells, it is much more richly ornamented, though in the same style. Just as the Romans used little frontons of temples, to adorn windows and niches, so the Buddhists employed little façades of Chaityas as ornaments, either over their doors or niches. The string course also, though this is not at first sight so obvious, is in reality of purely wooden construction. It is nothing more than wooden posts and rails repeated in stone, as may be seen at a glance at Sanchi, and other places where it is used on a larger scale. On this side of the hall, at the top is also seen the same form of battlement which is so frequently represented in the sculptures of Nineveh, but of which no ancient example exists (so far as is now known) in ^Hindostan.

VIHARA No. 11, AT AJUNTA.

———

NEXT in age to the last described is No. 11, very similar to the last in interior arrangement, but rather smaller, its length being 37 feet, its width only 28 feet 6 inches. Notwithstanding this it has four pillars supporting the roof, very clumsily introduced, and probably the first example of supports being so used, though afterwards their introduction became the rule, not the exception.

The external façade is plain, but in good taste, consisting of four plain octagonal piers with bracket capitals, standing in a plain panelled stylobate approached by a flight of steps ; the whole design being very appropriate to its position.

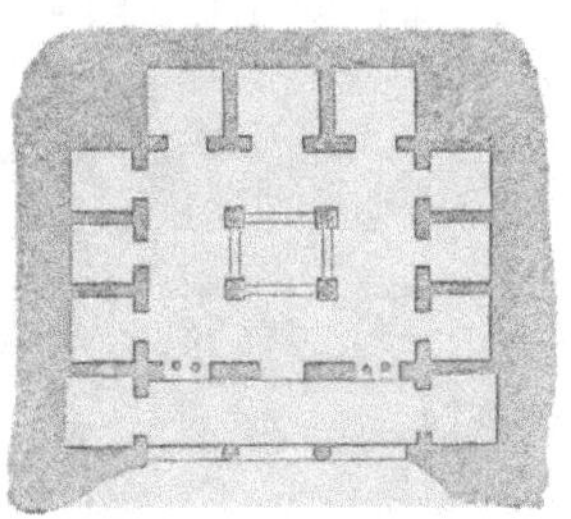

PLAN OF VIHARA NO. 11.
SCALE 50 FEET TO 1 INCH.

VERANDAH OF CAVE No. 11.—AJUNTA.

———

INTERNALLY the roof of the verandah has been painted, though probably at an age subsequent to the excavation, and is now very much obliterated. Its paintings, however, possess no historical interest, as they consist only of architectural patterns and borders, exhibiting what might be called a mixture of Classic and Assyrian designs.

The doorway leading to the interior is simple, and the steps are adorned with two lions' heads of good design, and well executed.

On either side is a large square window, separated into three lights by two pillars standing on the cills. These are square for the greater part of their height, but change into octagons and then into figures of sixteen sides, returning to the square form just below the capitals. This being to a greater or less extent the mode of decoration adopted for all pillars, not only at Ajunta, but in every part of India, so long as anything like a pure Hindoo style prevailed.

EXTERIOR OF VIHARA No. 14.—AJUNTA.

NUMBER 13 is a small cave situate high up the rock with only two cells, and nothing worthy of remark either in its arrangements or its architecture. Under it a large Vihara, No. 14, has been commenced, as if to form a lower storey, but at what age is not very clear, as for some reason it has been left unfinished, and it possesses no sculptures and no paintings from which an opinion as to its age can be deduced. The details of its pillars are peculiar, so much so, indeed, that there is no similar example known to exist elsewhere from which even an approximate date can be ascertained. Their style, however, is so pure and good, and there is no reason to doubt that they are of the age their position in the series would indicate, and rank among the oldest examples of Cave architecture.

INTERIOR OF VERANDAH No. 14.—AJUNTA.

THE form of the pillars of the verandah are square, divided by three flat bands forming compartments which are fluted exactly as is seen at the old Louvre or Tuileries, and other examples of Renaissance, but above this they slope inwards in a manner peculiar to Indian architecture. This form was adopted by the Hindoos in order that the abacus of the capital should not extend beyond the diameter of the shaft. In other words it was a device by which they obtained a pillar with a well marked capital out of a straight lined block of stone, with the least waste of material. As will be seen in the view, the two pillars at the end of the verandah are prepared to be so adorned.

The inner wall is arranged in a similar manner to that of all the Viharas here, but is more than usually plain, though this may arise from its being unfinished, or from its having been covered with chunam, and painted, but these adornments have perished, as is the case in almost all the verandahs at Ajunta.

VIHARA No. 15.—AJUNTA.

NUMBER 15 is a small plain Cave, the interior of which was till very recently filled up with mud, which had washed in from a torrent above, so as to render it inaccessible. To the same cause it' may perhaps be ascribed that the pillars of the verandah have fallen down and been obliterated. This Cave has now apparently been cleaned out, but no description of it has reached this country; and owing to the causes abovementioned, its external appearance presents nothing remarkable, except the sculpture of its doorway, which appears to have been executed with considerable care, and in a good style of art.

VIHARA No. 16.—AJUNTA.

NUMBERS 16 and 17 are the two most interesting Caves at Ajunta,—
in so far as painting is concerned, the most so in India.

No. 16, represented in the above view, is a square cave, 67 ft. 6 in. wide,
and 65 ft. 2 in. deep, exclusive of the sanctuary. The centre hall is surrounded
by twenty pillars, generally of an octagonal form, the sides of which are
adorned in painting with something like a Roman scroll, alternating with
wreaths of flowers.

All the details of the architecture of this Cave are particularly good and
elegant, more so than any other in this series. There are no side chapels, but
eighteen cells surrounding the great hall. The figure in the sanctuary is seated
with his feet down. Some of the paintings are tolerably entire and extremely
interesting, though not so much so as those in the next cave. Most of these
have been copied by Major Gill in facsimile, and these copies are now
exhibited in the Indian Court of the Crystal Palace at Sydenham.

17

VERANDAH OF CAVE No. 16.—AJUNTA.

T^HE verandah of this Cave, No. 16, is supported by plain octagonal columns with bracket capitals, not unlike those of No. 11, and its roof is ornamented with paintings of singularly elegant design, but which unfortunately have been very much destroyed by exposure to atmospheric influences.

There are no inscriptions in the Caves Nos. 16 and 17, which would enable us to fix their date with certainty, but from such data as exist, and such analogies as are available for comparison in other Caves, there can be little doubt but that they belong to the seventh or eighth centuries. At all events we cannot be mistaken if we assert that they were excavated and painted between what in Europe we should call the age of Justinian and that of Charlemagne, but probably nearer the age of the first than second-named emperor.

The doorway leading into the central hall is unusually plain, being merely adorned with one pilaster similar in design to the pillar in the verandah of Cave No. 11.

EXTERIOR OF VIHARA No. 17.—AJUNTA.

NUMBER 17, or, as it is generally called, the Zodiac Cave, very much resembles the last described in almost every respect. Its dimensions are 64 ft. by 63 ft. and it has twenty pillars disposed in the same manner as in the other. It is not, however, so lofty, and the details of the pillars are by no means so graceful or well designed as in No. 16. The paintings which adorn every part of the Vihara are much more entire than in any other cave of the series, and though the colours in some places are a good deal faded, they are preserved to such an extent at least that their subjects can generally be made out.

The pillars of the verandah, like most of those of the age, are plain octagons with bracket capitals, but their bases in this Cave are more elegant than usual.

VERANDAH OF CAVE No. 17.—AJUNTA.

AT the end of the verandah in this view is dimly seen the circular painting or so called zodiac, from which this Vihara derives its name. A facsimile of it is now at the Crystal Palace, Sydenham. It evidently represents terrestial scenes, divided into compartments by the spokes of a wheel, which always was a favourite emblem with Buddhists. The roof of the verandah is also very beautifully adorned with paintings, which are still in very perfect preservation, not unlike those found in the baths of Titus at Rome in design, but of course inferior in execution.

Over the door are painted eight figures sitting cross-legged. The first four are black, the fifth fairer, the next still more so, the last as fair as an European, and wearing a crown. It may be remarked that there are more black people represented in this cave than in any other ; the women, however, are generally fair, but the men are of all shades, from jet black to an European complexion.

AISLE IN HALL OF VIHARA No. 17.—AJUNTA.

A VIEW in the interior of Vihara No. 17, representing the first row of pillars internally from the entrance.

The two immediately in front of the doorway are as elegant as any pillars at Ajunta. The corresponding pair facing them opposite the sanctuary are richer but less graceful. The remaining sixteen are plain octagons with bracket capitals and no bases, but all richly painted. The figures of fat boys who do duty as transverse brackets supporting the beams of the roof, are peculiar to this Cave, though the wooden construction of the roof itself is the same in all, and is identical with that now used throughout India. In this instance it is of course repeated in the rock.

The great interest of this Cave is centered in the frescoes which cover every part of its interior ; those of the roof in geometrical patterns like those of the verandah, and those of the walls representing legendary scenes from the life of Buddha and other celebrated Buddhist worthies.

PORCH OF CHAITYA No. 19.—AJUNTA.

T HIS and the next eleven views are devoted to the Chaitya Cave No. 19, which is by far the richest and most complete of those in this series, perhaps the most so in India. It is not large, however, being only 46 ft. 4 in. by 23 ft. 7 in. in width, the nave being surrounded by only seventeen pillars; but it has scarcely suffered at all from the hand of time, and all its ornaments being sculptured, they remain as distinct at the present day as when first executed.

There is nothing to fix with certainty the age of this Cave. It is certainly later than the Viharas last described, and cotemporary with some of those which follow, while there are analogies and other circumstances which cannot be detailed here, which render it probable that it was excavated about the eighth century of our era.

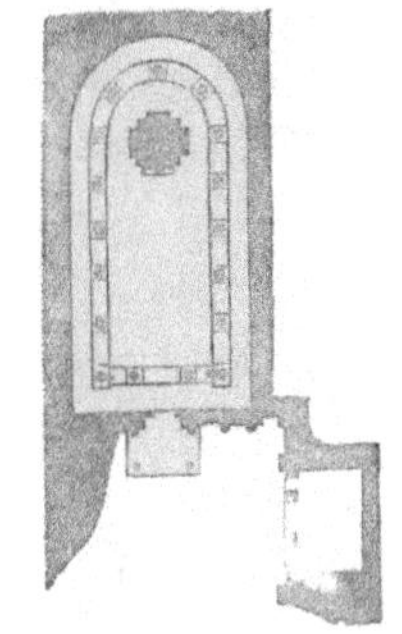

PLAN OF CHAITYA NO. 19.
SCALE, 50 FEET TO 1 INCH.

GREAT WINDOW OF CHAITYA No. 19.—AJUNTA.

R EPRESENTS the upper part of the façade, the lower or entrance part of
which was shown in the last view. It shows the same general arrangement as the first Cave described ; but, as will be observed, the purely wooden
decorations have become considerably modified in the course of time. The
niches and little semicircular canopies have lost so much of their wooden origin
that, if they could not be traced back, their derivation would hardly be suspected,
The wooden forms, however, still remain the same on the inner face of the
great arch, and in the overhanging part of the rock which crowns the façade.
This shows the same beam and rafter arrangement as the verandah of the last
Vihara described, and is, indeed, universal throughout India.

LOWER PART OF FACADE OF CHAITYA No. 19.—AJUNTA.

T^HIS view represents the sculpture on the right-hand side of the lower part of the façade of Chaitya Cave No. 19.   The principal figure on the right hand of the entrance represents Buddha giving alms.   In the next compartment he is standing in front of a daghopa, richly ornamented and surmounted by the triple umbrella, standing on the tee, which is so universal an emblem in these times, and is, in fact, merely a repetition of what is seen inside the Cave itself.   Above, on the upper right-hand corner of the picture, he is represented, in the most usual standing attitude, as preaching, his right hand hanging down, his left raised ; but the style of the sculpture is so far inferior as to lead to the suspicion of a later date.   Below this he is represented seated cross-legged, but this also is in an inferior style of art.

LOWER PART OF FACADE OF CHAITYA No. 19.—AJUNTA.

O N the left of the entrance, as you look towards it, Buddha is represented
standing in the usual attitude of exposition. In the next compartment
he is seated cross-legged over a shrine, in the front of which is another figure
of himself standing under a very rich canopy. Beyond these are repetitions
of the same two figures as bounded the composition in the last view, but in
this position they are apparently in the same style of art as the central compartments, and range much better with the architectural composition than they
do on the other side. Beyond, on the extreme left, is seen the commencement of the Hindoo shrine described further on as No. 33.

The two pillars which support the porch, and the pilasters which separate
these various sculptured groups, are all covered with the most elaborate orna-
mentation, as delicate in execution as any found at Ajunta, and generally in
better preservation than such sculptures usually are in positions equally exposed,

INTERIOR OF CHAITYA No. 19.—AJUNTA.

VIEW taken from the entrance showing the arrangement of the interior and illustrating also the effect of the mode of lighting. The whole light being introduced through one great opening in the centre of the façade throws a brilliant light on the altar—the principal object—and also in the triforium belt and the capitals of the pillars, being exactly where it is most wanted for artistic effect. The spectator himself stands in the shade. The light on the floor is subdued, and the roof and aisles fade into comparative gloom. It is perhaps the most artistic mode of lighting a building of this class that has ever been invented, certainly superior to anything that was done by the Romans, or during the middle ages. It might require the brilliant climate of India to admit of its application to any large hall; but, for a small chapel or room, the one great light behind and above the worshippers is the most perfect arrangement which has yet been attempted.

ROOF OF CHAITYA, No. 19.—AJUNTA.

VIEW taken from the upper gallery, showing the construction of the roof, which still retains the wooden forms of ribs with a ridge piece, though being cut in the rock they are probably stouter and thicker than they were when really executed in timber. The upper part of the daghopa is also seen, with its three umbrellas, but these have departed still further from their wooden prototypes, and are fast approaching those forms which gave rise to the three, six, and nine-storied towers of the Jains, and which are still built at the present day in China. The connexion between the porcelain tower at Nankin, and a hemispherical dome surmounted by a wooden umbrella, is certainly not at first sight apparent; but there are few things more clear than that the one is the direct lineal descendant of the other, and every step of the change can be pointed out.

TRIFORIUM OF CHAITYA, No. 19.—AJUNTA.

THIS and the three following views represent four different portions of the triforium belt of the Cave No. 19, and form as rich a piece of sculptured decoration as is to be found in any Buddhist cave in India, though many may be purer and in better taste.

It is also interesting as illustrating the process of change from painting to carving which took place in India as in the middle ages in our own country, and probably also in Greece. The Romanesque architects left all their masonry plain in great flat surfaces as in Cave No. 10. The Gothic artists, on the contrary, trusted very little to colour, but depended chiefly on relief for their shadow and effects.

So far as can be made out, the subjects painted in Cave No. 10 were very much the same as those represented here, but have perished in consequence of the less durable materials in which they were executed.

TRIFORIUM OF CHAITYA, No. 19.—AJUNTA.

A S will be seen in all those interior views, the whole surface was covered with a thin coating of chunam so as entirely to hide the surface of the rock ; but the sculptors never seem to have thought that this could excuse them from using the same amount of elaboration in their carving as if they were to be left plain.   Though it may be supposed they were prepared in this way for the purpose of being painted, it does not appear that any colour was in this instance applied.

There is not much variety in the sculptures of the triforium belt itself. These consist of alternate sitting and standing figures of Buddha.   The sitting ones all cross-legged, the only variety being in the position of the hands, to which Buddhists attach much importance.   Between each of these is a standing figure in the usual attitude of exposition, and though the attitude in all is very nearly the same, no two figures are exactly alike, and the variations have probably more meaning than is apparent to the casual observer.

TRIFORIUM OF CHAITYA No. 19.—AJUNTA.

GREAT richness of effect is given to this interior by the elaborate sculptures of the capitals. These consist, in every instance, of a square niche containing a seated figure of Buddha, only very slightly varied. The brackets on either side of the central block differ every one from the other, and consist of figures of men and women in the most violent attitudes; of men on horseback, or elephants, of griffins, and dragons—in short, a whole legendary history of Buddhism and of Buddhist symbolism, for there cannot be a doubt but that each composition had a legend attached to it, though we can now only identify a very few of these fragmentary groups. Indeed, we can hardly feel certain that we know the subject of all the larger and more circumstantial pictures painted on the walls of the Viharas.

TRIFORIUM OF CHAITYA No. 19.—AJUNTA.

T^{HE} spaces between the figure-sculptures are filled in with scrolls, in the triforium belt, of the usual patterns of the age. As a matter of course they are all different, and show a considerable amount of design and elaboration. ^Human masks, and dragons' heads, and other fantastic devices, are frequently mixed with the foliage, and add considerably to the effect. They, too, are evidently all copied from painted originals, and have not in this instance attained that architectural formality which they afterwards acquired, and which is so essential to true architectural effect.

The shafts of the pillars of the nave are also covered with sculptured ornaments, but as these were essential constructive parts of the building, the ornament on them is of a much soberer and more architectural form, and never interferes with the outline or the constructive effect of the columns it ornaments.

CHOULTRIE ATTACHED TO CHAITYA No. 19.—AJUNTA.

O N the right-hand side, as you enter, is a small porch, extending at right angles to the main façade. This is not a Vihara, or residence, but a Choultrie, or place of refuge or repose for pilgrims or attendants.

The front consists of two pillars of very graceful design, and the whole composition is pleasing and appropriate to its purposes.

It may be of the same age as the Chaitya to which it belongs, and form a part of its original arrangements, but there is a certain character about the sculpture of its capitals which would lead us to suspect that it was added afterwards at some more modern date.

If this is not so, it may be considered as one of the very earliest examples of a mode of changing a circular form into a square one, by a leaf falling over at the angles. It is somewhat clumsily used here, but afterwards became universal in Indian architecture.

HINDOO SCULPTURE. CHAITYA No. 19.—AJUNTA.

OPPOSITE to the Choultrie last described is an alto-relievo of a considerably more modern date than the Chaitya to which it is attached, and
probably the only thing that can be ascribed to the Brahmans at Ajunta.

It represents Vishnu sitting under the canopy of the seven-headed snake—
a very common Brahmanical arrangement—with Sareswati by his side. On
the other side stands an attendant with a chowrie in his hand.

Though more modern than the Chaitya, it is not necessary to assume that this
group was carved after the Caves were deserted. There were intervals long
before the final expulsion of the Buddhists, when the Brahmans had the upper
hand, and this piece of sculpture is so free from the usual extravagance of
Hindoo sculpture, that it must be old—older probably than the Caves at either
end of the series.

In style, it resembles very much the sculptures at Elephanta, and some of
those at Ellora.

33

CAVE No. 20.—AJUNTA.

THE last of this group is a small Vihara of somewhat singular plan. Its dimensions are twenty-eight feet two inches wide, by twenty-five feet six inches deep. It possesses four cells for monks, two on each side. There is no internal colonnade, but the roof is supported by advancing the sanctuary about seven feet into the hall and making its front consist of two columns in antis.

There is also a verandah in front, supported by two pillars with bracket capitals. The sculpture of these is bold and free, resembling that of the capitals in the interior of Cave No. 19, though somewhat better executed. Unfortunately, like everything in this Cave, the façade is a good deal ruined from flaws and faults in the rock.

CAVE No. 20.—AJUNTA.

THE paintings that once adorned this Cave are now almost entirely obliterated, except those on the roof. Those which exist consist of frets and flowers, but do not possess any particular interest beyond showing the connexion of this Cave with the Viharas 16 and 17, whose paintings are identical in style.

This Cave has been used as a workshop and occasional residence by Major Gill during the twenty years he has remained at Ajunta, and were it not for the difficulty of procuring sufficient light in the interior, there can be no doubt but that their dryness and equable temperature would render these caves very pleasant places to live in.

With this Cave the great central group terminates in this direction ; and it will now be necessary to describe the third group, consisting of the first seven Caves in the north, and then to take up the fourth, though probably cotemporary group, consisting of the last six at the southern end.

FACADE CAVE No. 7.—AJUNTA.

———

NUMBER 7 is peculiar among the Caves of Ajunta, though not unlike some at Cuttack.

It consists merely of a large verandah 63 ft. 4 in. in length, by 13 ft. 7 in. in breadth, with the cells opening at the back of it. The front line of the verandah is broken by the projection of two porches, of two pillars each. These are particularly interesting here, as they are extremely similar to the pillars at Elephanta, and those in the Doomar Lena at Ellora, and therefore probably not far distant in date. There is also a chapel with two pillars at each end of the verandah.

Though it cannot pretend to rival in magnificence some of the other Viharas at Ajunta, as an architectural composition it is probably as pleasing as any others—externally at least.

CAVE No. 6.—AJUNTA.

NUMBER 6 is the only two-storied Cave at Ajunta, but has unfortunately been excavated in a spot where the rock is not so sound as in other places. In consequence of this the verandah of the upper storey has fallen down, and the interior has a damp and ruined aspect, not common in Cave architecture.

The halls of both stories are of the same dimensions, 53 ft. square, the upper having twelve pillars. In the lower, four more are introduced in the centre.

The pillars in front of the sanctuary are of the same Elephanta order as in the last described Cave, with cushion capitals, and fluted.

It will be observed in the above view of the facade there was a figure standing in the nook shaft on each side of the doorway, but it has fallen away, its absence giving an awkward appearance to the design.

FACADE CAVE No. 5.—AJUNTA.

NUMBER 5 is a small Cave with no remarkable peculiarity about it, and
unfinished, so that it is impossible to be quite certain of its age, but
as the series of Caves seem to have gradually extended from the central groups
towards the extremities, it may probably rank next in time to the last
described. On careful examination, however, it will be seen that its pillars,
though of the same order as the next in succession, No. 4, are so inferior in
design that it may probably be an insertion of a later date, and its unfinished
state would also lead to the supposition that it may be among those last
attempted at this place.

FACADE OF CAVE No. 4.—AJUNTA.

THE fourth Cave from the end is situated higher up in the cliff than the others at this end of the series, and as the path to it has broken away, it was so completely hid from below by the ledge in front of it, that I was not aware of its existence till I perceived it from the opposite side of the valley when leaving—too late to return. I have therefore no dimensions and no such intimate knowledge of it as would enable me to speak confidently either as to its age or any of its arrangements. This is the more to be regretted as, both from its dimensions as well as from the simple grandeur of its details, it looks as if it were one of the finest Viharas of the series.

INTERIOR OF VERANDA^H, CAVE No. 4.—AJUNTA.

THE verandah of this Cave is supported apparently by eight pillars in front ; simple octagons with bracket capitals, but without bases, or any inter-mediate member to break the abruptness of the change between the capital and the shaft, but the whole is massive and plain, and consequently appropriate to Cave architecture ; more so indeed than many of the more elaborate designs which are found in this as well in all the other groups of Caves, more especially among those so modern as this one evidently is.

SCULPTURE IN VERANDAH OF CAVE No. 4.—AJUNTA.

THE wall at the back of the verandah is sculptured instead of being painted, which is unusual at Ajunta, and an evidence for the modern date of the excavation. The style of the sculpture, too, has more of the character we are accustomed to associate with Jaina than with Buddhist art. Its presence, however, gives a richness of effect to this verandah which is wanting in the others, where the paintings have been washed off, from the exposed nature of the situation.

EXTERIOR, CAVE No. 2.—AJUNTA.

THE second Cave from the north end is a twelve-pillared Vihara, of which is given a plan at page xviii. It is in very good preservation, and the paintings, particularly on the pillars, are tolerably perfect. In the sanctuary there is a statue, of course of Buddha, and there is a chapel on each side of it, at the end of the aisles. In the one on the north are two most portly, fat figures, a male and female; in the south one, two male figures occupying a like position. Who they were meant to represent is by no means clear.

Though the dimensions of its hall are only 48 ft. square, and its age very modern (ninth or tenth century probably), it is as complete an example of a perfect Vihara as any existing in Ajunta or elsewhere.

VERANDAH, CAVE No. 2.—AJUNTA.

———

THE verandah is supported by four pillars of very massive form and tolerably elegant design. The lower portion is of sixteen sides, above this they are adorned with thirty-two flutes; but their principal ornaments are arranged in the belts which surround them. These are covered with the most elegant ornaments, so delicate as to be almost better suited for metal than for stone work. At either end of it a smaller porch stands in front of the two principal cells, the difference in height being made up by bassi-relievi representing scenes from the life of Buddha. The doorway leading into the hall is also a rich and elegant specimen of its class.

VERANDA^H, CAVE No. 2.—AJUNTA.

T HE principal effect of this Cave is derived from its paintings, especially those on the ceiling. These are not of the same high class of historical paintings which adorn the Viharas 16 and 17, being generally only
decorative scrolls and patterns, but as architectural ornaments, they are more
complete and elaborate than those found in the other Caves, and being
generally appropriate to the situation in which they are placed, they give a
greater effect of finish to this Cave than is usual at Ajunta. Taken altogether, there is perhaps no Cave at this place from which the effect and
arrangements of a complete Vihara can be better understood than they can
from this example.

FACADE, CAVE No. 1.—AJUNTA.

THE first Cave that begins, or rather ends, ^{the} series in the northerly direction, possesses the most highly ornamented, perhaps it might be said, the handsomest exterior of all the Viharas of Ajunta.   The hall of its interior is 64 feet square, adorned with twenty pillars, each 3 ft. in diameter, all of them richly carved, and with bold bracket capitals.

The interior has been a good deal filled with mud, but notwithstanding this, its paintings are tolerably entire, and some of them are interesting, but like the sculpture and all the details of the architecture, they are small, and frittered away, and possess nothing of that breadth of treatment which characterizes some of the older excavations.

FACADE, CAVE No. 1.—AJUNTA.

T_{HE} verandah of this Cave is 98 ft. in length internally, and terminates as usual in a cell at each end, but externally it has, besides, a chapel, with two pillars in antis, which adds considerably to the architectural effect of the façade, and in this respect is preferable to the arrangement in No. 2, where these two pillars are internal, and consequently are hardly seen in conjunction with the façade.

As originally executed, there was an outer porch of two pillars standing in advance of the six which are still perfect. These latter, which form the real support of the verandah, are of three different orders—or rather four, counting the half columns at either end. The outer pillars are merely square piers, but they increase in richness of decoration from the flanks to the centre, where they are richly decorated circular shafts, with bold bracket capitals.

FACADE, CAVE No. 1.—AJUNTA.

THE two central pillars of the six which remain have circular shafts, with perpendicular flutings in bands, sixteen-sided above and below, and thirty-two in the two middle compartments.

The two next on either hand have diagonal flutings, and less ornament at the top and bottom.

The two beyond these are comparatively plain octagons, with only slight ornamental markings, and the half columns are square, with only a circular necking below the square block of the capital. All these pillars, however, have bracket capitals of similar design, though the sculpture in each is varied. The whole effect is that of a well considered and carefully elaborated design, though, perhaps, hardly so appropriate to rock architecture as the design of No. 4, and some of the simpler Caves of the series.

FACADE, CAVE No. 1.—AJUNTA.

IT is not easy to make out the design of the two advanced columns in the centre. From what remains we can see that they had not bracket capitals, but were similar to those of the Cave last described (No. 2), but the double frieze of sculpture was carried round them as along the whole façade, binding it together as a whole.

Taking it altogether, this façade is perhaps as pleasing a specimen of design as is to be found in this style of architecture. If the principles on which it is composed are condemned, the whole system falls; but it seems there is an amount of variety combined with sufficient uniformity for architectural purposes, and there is a richness of effect produced by the whole composition, for which it would not be easy to quote a rival in any other building of the same size or pretensions.

INTERIOR OF VERANDAH, CAVE No. I.—AJUNTA.

I NTERNALLY the verandah does not present so pleasing an aspect at the
present day as the exterior, in consequence of its having depended for
effect principally on paintings, and these have perished.

Owing to the shadows, the internal photograph shows better than those of
the exterior the system on which these pillars are designed. First, a square
cubical base, the same height for all. On this an octagonal frustrum of a
shaft also uniform in height. The transition being broken by a seated figure
at each angle. In the centre pillars this changes into a sixteen-sided figure at
top and bottom. In the next two only at the top, on the outside ones not at all ;
but all have belts of thirty-two sides in the centres,—the same system being
observable not only throughout their architecture, but in every phase of
H indoo thought or design.

DOORWAY, CAVE No. 1.—AJUNTA.

THE doorway is hardly so rich as might be expected in so elaborately ornamented a Cave, but it is pleasing in design, and as it was covered with chunam, traces of which still remain, it is probable that its effect was at one time heightened by colour. Besides this, it must be remembered that it is only one feature in what once was a richly decorated wall, and if so, it showed correct architectural taste to keep it subdued. A richly sculptured design in bold relief would have tended to render the flat paintings on either hand, tame and insipid.

Two of the internal pillars can be seen dimly through the opening. They are similar in design to those of the exterior. As before mentioned, there are twenty of these, each three feet in diameter.

VERANDA^H, CAVE No. 21.--AJUNTA.

RETURNING to the southern end, the next Cave (No. 21) is a large Vihara 51 ft. 6 in. by 52 ft. 6 in. but not quite finished, the pillars of the sanctuary being merely blocked out.

In style and detail it is very similar to the Cave No. 2, at the other end, showing the same exuberance of ornament, but with the same weakness of design and detail.

Besides the sanctuary, there are four chapels in this Cave, one on each side and one at each end of the two aisles, and all of these have two pillars in antis. Their frequency, and the mode in which they have superseded the residential cells, show only too clearly how the original idea of the Vihara was becoming lost at the time when this one was excavated.

Two chapels at the ends of the verandah still also remain, one of which is represented in the above view, and though the pillars of the front of the verandah are gone, the end pier on both sides remains, marking its dimensions and showing the character of its details.

DOORWAY, CAVE No. 21.—AJUNTA.

THE doorway that leads into the Cave No. 21 has the same elegance, but the same littleness as all the other parts of this Vihara, and with a tendency towards Hindooism indicative of its modern date. It is still however, so free from the extravagance that too generally prevailed in Indian architecture, after the tenth or eleventh century, that there can be no doubt about its being earlier than that epoch.

Internally its paintings are now nearly obliterated, except on the wall on your left hand as you enter, where there still exists a large figure of Buddha, of a black complexion, or at least very dark, but with red hair, and attended by black slaves. There are several ladies introduced into the composition, but notwithstanding the blackness of their companions they are here, as in most other Caves, represented with complexions almost as fair as Europeans.

CAVE No. 22.--AJUNTA.

T_{HE} Vihara No. 22 is a small Cave, only 17 ft. square, without pillars except two, which are merely rough hewn, in front of the sanctuary. The whole Cave, in fact, has the appearance of having been left unfinished internally, and whatever external decoration it may once have had, is now lost, owing to the façade having fallen down from the decay of the rock in which it was sculptured.

It is now used as a residence, if not by Major Gill himself, at least by his followers, whose portraits are seen in the photograph. Their various ranks and stations will be easily recognised by any one familiar with an Indian household, from the fierce jemadar, who is attitudinizing on the right, to the mehtur boy, who is sitting with his back against the door-jamb on the left.

FAÇADE, CAVE No. 23.—AJUNTA.

<hr>

NUMBER 23 is another Vihara of twelve pillars, very similar in all respects to Nos. 2 and 21 ; it has however been left in a very unfinished state, without even an image either in the sanctuary, or indeed anywhere else, and there exists no trace of painting that could be detected in any part.   Its dimensions are 51 ft. by 51 ft. 8 in.

The pillars of its external façade are bold and suitable in design to rock-cut architecture ; but they are deficient in elegance of outline, and their details are small and shallow to an extent wholly unsuited to their position.

It was probably intended to flute the centre pillars like those on the flanks ; but they, like everything else, are left unfinished.

VERANDAH, CAVE No. 23.—AJUNTA.

———

THE unfinished interior of this Cave and the next one (No. 24) are interesting as showing the whole process by which these Caves were excavated. In one place, what was to be a range of pillars is a wall rock roughly blocked out with a pick. In another it is pierced with what look like a series of rude doorways. In some places the pillars are shaped, in others the carving is finished. On the whole, it appears that it is the last process that has taken the greatest amount of time and labour. The blocking out of a Cave in such a material as amygdaloidal trap is probably not a more expensive process than building such a structure on the plain might prove. If this be so, the durability of a rock-cut structure is such that it might have been far more generally adopted were it not that the situation where they are necessarily placed is often inconvenient, and the power of lighting them frequently insufficient.

FACADE, No. 24.—AJUNTA.

NUMBER 24 was intended to have been a twenty-pillared Cave, and, if finished, would have measured about 74 ft. each way. But only one pillar in the interior is sculptured, and one range exists only as a wall, with slits in it.

The pillars of the verandah have been finished, but not the friezes, which no doubt were intended to crown them, judging from the mass of plain rock that is left over them, as if for that purpose.

From such details as exist, we may infer that, if completed, this would have been one of the most carefully finished Caves of the series.

In the pillars of the verandah we have another instance of the falling-leaf ornament which became so fashionable at Delhi and elsewhere, in the eleventh and twelfth centuries, and which occurs also in the Choultrie to Cave No. 19, which may probably be of the same age.

Though so rare at Ajunta, the falling-leaf ornament is almost universal at Ellora, as will be seen in the illustrations that follow.

56

LOWER PART OF FACADE AT CHAITYA No. 26.—AJUNTA.

———

T^HOUG^H there are some insignificant Caves-beyond, the great Chaitya
No. 26 terminates the series as worthily at this end as the Vihara
No. 1, does at the other.

In general plan it is very similar to No. 19, but its dimensions exceed the
former very considerably, the whole width being 36 ft. 3 ins., that of the nave
17 ft. 7 ins., and the total length is 66 ft. 1 in.   Its sculptures, too, are far more
numerous and more elaborate ; indeed, more so than in any other Cave of the
series ; but they are very inferior both in design and in execution, so much so,
that if other proof were wanting, this alone would be sufficient to stamp this
at once as one of the latest, if not actually the last executed Cave of Ajunta.

UPPER PART OF FACADE, No. 26.—AJUNTA.

T_{HE} external architecture has nearly lost all trace of its wooden origin, except the rafters of the great opening, which were seldom lost sight of ; but now they are beginning to be used as shelves for figures, and the lowest is cut through to make room for two seated Buddhas, larger than the rest.

The whole of the roof of the external porch or music gallery in front has fallen in, but so far as can be made out, it extended the whole way across, which is unusual at Ajunta.

Internally the walls of the aisles, instead of being painted, are covered with sculptures, among them a reclining figure of Buddha, 23 ft. long, in the attitude in which Nirvana or beatitude is attained.   But this is accompanied by figures so comical and extravagant in design, as prove too clearly that the religion of Sakya Muni no longer existed in its original purity when the Cave was undertaken.

THE

CAVES OF ELLORA.

INTRODUCTION.

ALTHOUGH the caves at Ellora do not possess that unity and completeness which characterises those of Ajunta, their variety, and the exceptional magnificence of some of them, renders them perhaps even more interesting : but it must be confessed they are in consequence far more difficult to understand. It is only, indeed, after having become familiar with all the other forms of Cave architecture, that their history becomes at all intelligible.

It is not, therefore, to be wondered at that such strange theories were announced with regard to their age and uses when they were first made known to Europeans ; for, beside their complexity, it also happened that the Ellora Caves were the earliest series of which any trustworthy illustrations were published, and they consequently attracted attention at a time when very few materials existed for forming a judgment regarding their peculiarities. Very correct views of them were published by the Daniels, from drawings made by Wales, in the first years of this century; and the writings of Seely, of Colonel Sykes, and Sir Charles Mallet, have all contributed to make them known ; but unfortunately none of these gentlemen were familiar—at the time they wrote—with the other forms of Cave architecture, and they were consequently unable to classify them correctly as to either age or style.

The whole series consists of about thirty excavations. Of these ten were devoted to the religion of Buddha, fourteen were excavated by the followers of the Brahmanical creeds, and six cannot be said to belong to either of these sects; nor can they in strictness be ascribed to the Jains, though their sculpture savours more of the tenets of their religion than those of the other two.

Architecturally the Ellora Caves differ from those of Ajunta in consequence of their being excavated in the sloping sides of a hill, and not in a nearly perpendicular cliff. From this formation of the ground almost all the caves at Ellora have courtyards in front of them. Frequently also, an outer wall of rock with an entrance through it is left standing, so that the caves are not generally seen from the outside at all, and a person might pass along their front without being aware of their existence unless warned of the fact. On the other hand, the advantage architecturally of the fore-court, and the protection it affords not only from violence, but also from atmospheric influences, more than compensate for this defect.

EXTERIOR VISWAKARMA.—ELLORA.

O F the Buddhist group, the principal Cave is the so-called Viswakarma, the only Chaitya Cave of the series. It is neither so large as those of Karli or Salsette, being only 43 ft. wide internally, and 83 ft. 1 in. in length ; nor is it so rich in its details as the two later Chaityas at Ajunta.

Internally the design of the Temple is marked with considerable elegance and simplicity. The two pillars that support the gallery over the entrance are rich and handsome ; the twenty-eight others are simple octagons, changing for a short portion of their height into a figure of sixteen sides.

In front of the daghopa is Buddha seated with his feet down, and surrounded by flying figures and Genii, savouring much more of Brahmanism than the purer religion of the Ascetic, and throughout the whole of the interior the sculptures are much more secular than in any other Buddhist excavation. The alteration in style, in fact, is so obvious, as to prove that the religion of Buddha had lost all its primitive force and originality before this Cave was excavated, and was fast merging into these religions that superseded it.

www.ingramcontent.com/pod-product-compliance
Lightning Source LLC
LaVergne TN
LVHW021643160726
843514LV00001B/2